Thank you for purchase the book. I hope it has been helpful.
More of my products you will find on:

https://amzn.to/3dICQMj

Copyright © 2021 by Suellen Palove

For more information, address: suellen.palove@gmail.com

life is
too short
to wait.

Voucher

Foot massage

Can by redeemed only once!

love

life is too short to wait.

Voucher

Sexy striptease

Can by redeemed only once!

love

life is too short to wait.

Voucher

Quickie

Can by redeemed only once!

love

life is too short to wait.

Voucher

Breakfast in bed

Can by redeemed only once!

love

life is too short to wait.

Voucher

Role play

Can by redeemed only once!

love

life is too short to wait.

Voucher

Dirty dancing

Can by redeemed only once!

love

life is too short to wait.

Voucher

New position

Can by redeemed only once!

love

life is too short to wait.

Voucher

Car fun

Can by redeemed only once!

love

life is too short to wait.

Voucher

Private photoshoot

Can by redeemed only once!

love

life is too short to wait.

Voucher

Erotic movie night

Can by redeemed only once!

love

life is too short to wait.

Voucher

Use handcuffs

Can by redeemed only once!

love

life is too short to wait.

Voucher

A quickie in an unexpected place

Can by redeemed only once!

love

life is too short to wait.

Voucher

Act out a movie scene

Can by redeemed only once!

love

life is too short to wait.

Voucher

Steamy foreplay session

Can by redeemed only once!

love

life is too short to wait.

Voucher

Be a doctor

Can by redeemed only once!

love

life is too short to wait.

Voucher

2 new sex position

Can by redeemed only once!

love

life is
too short
to wait.

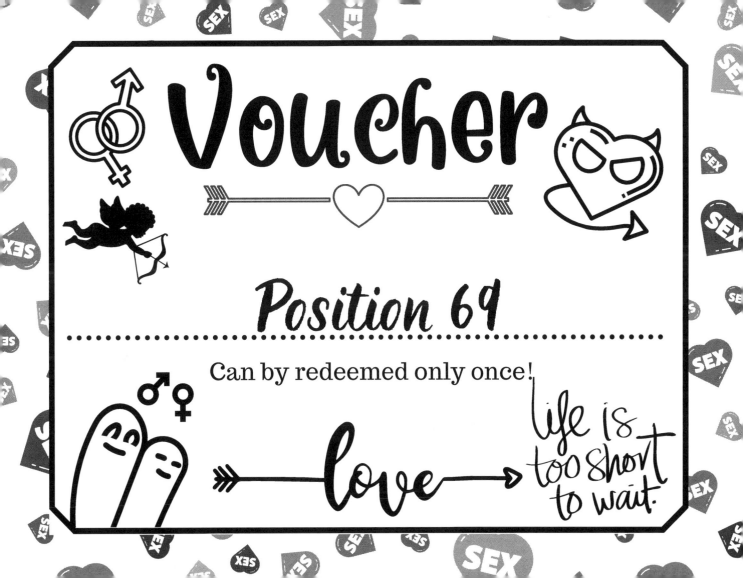

Voucher

Position 69

Can by redeemed only once!

love

life is too short to wait.

Voucher

Seductive phone sex

Can by redeemed only once!

love

life is too short to wait.

Voucher

Shower sex

Can by redeemed only once!

love

life is too short to wait.

Voucher

Dress me up

Can by redeemed only once!

love

life is too short to wait.

Voucher

Unlimited touching

Can by redeemed only once!

love

life is too short to wait.

Voucher

Sex by candlelight

Can by redeemed only once!

life is too short to wait.

Voucher

Meeting as strangers

Can by redeemed only once.

love

life is too short to wait.

Voucher

Seduce me

Can by redeemed only once!

life is too short to wait.

Voucher

Nude body massage

Can by redeemed only once!

love

life is too short to wait.

Voucher

Finger fun

Can by redeemed only once!

love

life is too short to wait.

Voucher

Blindfolded sex

Can by redeemed only once!

love

life is too short to wait.

Voucher

Make dinner in only an apron

Can by redeemed only once!

love

life is too short to wait.

Voucher

Write out what you'll do to me, then read it aloud

Can by redeemed only once!

love

life is too short to wait.

Voucher

Body painting

Can by redeemed only once!

love

life is too short to wait.

Voucher

Mattress wrestling

Can by redeemed only once!

love

life is too short to wait.

Voucher

Naked pillow fight

Can by redeemed only once!

love

life is too short to wait.

Voucher

Tickle tease

Can by redeemed only once!

love

life is too short to wait.

Voucher

Can by redeemed only once!

love

life is too short to wait.

Voucher

Can by redeemed only once!

love

life is too short to wait.

Voucher

Can by redeemed only once!

love

life is too short to wait.

Voucher

Can by redeemed only once!

love

life is too short to wait.

Voucher

Can by redeemed only once!

love

life is
too short
to wait.